HOW WE KNOW ABOUT
THE GREEKS

JOHN AND LOUISE JAMES

PETER BEDRICK BOOKS

ACKNOWLEDGEMENTS

The publishers would like to thank Robert Morkot for his advice and assistance in the preparation of this book, and the organizations that have given their permission to reproduce the following pictures:

Ancient Art & Architecture collection: 13 (jug).
Antikensammlung Staatliche Museen ze Berlin - Preussischer Kulturbesitz: 22 (drunks).
Bildarchiv Preussischer Kulturbesitz, Berlin: 17 (relief), 18 (bowl, bottom).
Courtesy of the Trustees of the British Museum: 6 (vase and tablet), 7 (coin),
8 (necklace), 9 (vase and model), 10 (vase), 12 (perfume pot), 17 (mirror and bowl),
18 (bowl, above), 19 (relief), 24 (Aphrodite), 26 (vase).
e.t.archive: 28 (quiver and shield).
Mary Evans Picture Library/Explorer: 29 (bust).
Michael Holford: 7 (relief), 16 (earring).
Courtesy Museum of Fine Arts, Boston: 11 (press), 11 (vase), 13 (model).
National Geographic Society Image Collection: 15 (pottery).
National Museum, Athens: 20 (votive relief), 21 (votive relief),
23 (comic mask), 24 (Athena), 26 (relief).
Scala: 25 (coin), 27 (wrestlers.)

Written by: Louise James
Illustrated by: John James
Editor: Andrew Farrow
Art Director: Cathy Tincknell
Design: John James and Joanna Malivoire
Consultant: Dr. Robert Morkot

Other titles in the series: *The Romans, The Vikings, The Egyptians*

Published by
PETER BEDRICK BOOKS
a division of NTC/Contemporary Publishing Group
4255 West Touhy Avenue
Lincolnwood (Chicago), Illinois 60712-1975 U.S.A.

Library of Congress Cataloging in Publication Data
James, John. 1959-
How we know about the Greeks / John and Louise James.
P. cm
Includes index.
Summary: Looks at some of the evidence for the ancient Greek way of life, including
archaeological research and the works of philosophers and playwrights.
ISBN 0-87226-537-4
1. Greece--Civilization--To 146 B.C.--Juvenile literature.
[1. Greece--Civilization--To 146 B.C.] I. James, Louise. II Title.
DF77.J34 1997
938--dc21

Second printing, 2000
Printed in Hong Kong

CONTENTS

SETTING THE SCENE

Greece 432 BC

The ancient Greek civilization existed over two thousand years ago. Its people lived in many small states on the mainland and islands of Greece, which they had inherited from the Minoans of Crete and the Mycenaeans. They also settled in new lands, called colonies, and traded mainly with neighbors to the south – the Egyptians and Syrians. Greek armies even defeated the might of the Persians.

One of the most powerful Greek states was Athens. All of the city's adult male citizens were allowed to cast a vote for who should be their leader. This system of government, which today we call democracy, was described by the Greek philosopher Aristotle in about 335 BC:

'The basis of a democratic state is liberty... the second characteristic of democracy... is for men to be ruled by none... or, if this is impossible, to rule and be ruled in turns.'

The timeline below shows the ancient Greeks in relation to some other important civilizations. This book looks mainly at the period 500-300 BC, when city-states such as Athens and Sparta were at their most powerful.

The map on the right shows the homelands and colonies of the ancient Greeks, some neighboring civilizations, and some of the important goods they traded.

Areas colonized by Greece
wine
wool
cloth
ivory
papyrus
iron
copper

GAUL

ADRIATIC SEA

Heracles
ITALY
Agatha
Antipons
CORSICA
Poseidonia
Elea
Syb
Massalia
Alalia
Emporion
SARDINIA
Himera
IBERIA
SICILY
Akra
BALEARIC ISLANDS
Carthage
NUMIDIA

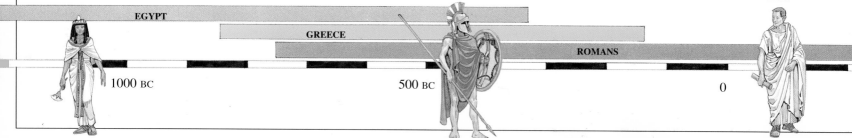

ABOUT 850 BC GREECE EMERGES FROM DARK AGES   ABOUT 753 BC FOUNDATION OF ROME   332 BC EGYPT FALLS TO ALEXANDER THE GREAT   140 BC GREECE FALLS TO ROMAN ARMIES

EGYPT

GREECE

ROMANS

1000 BC   500 BC   0

The scene on the left shows the statesman Pericles speaking to the citizens of Athens. Under his leadership, some of Athens' greatest buildings were erected, such as the Parthenon, seen in the background.

Theodosia

Olbia

Trapezos

Tyras

BLACK SEA

slaves

Tomis

Herakleia

Byzantion

ASIA MINOR

Poseidon

SYRIA

CEDONIA

Troy

PERSIA

Priene

(Kyrenia)

Salamis

Phaselis

CYPRUS

Sidon

GREECE

Marathon

Paphos

Tyre

Athens

AEGEAN

RHODES

Corinth

SEA

Olympia

Epidauros

Sparta

CRETE

Alexandria

Naukratis

ARABIA

perfume

EGYPT

MEDITERRANEAN SEA

RIVER
NILE

RED SEA

Kyrene

LIBYA

Euhesperides

Thebes

This type of government is just one of the legacies we have from the Greek age. Other ideas that we still follow today include going to the theater to see plays, styles of architecture, ways of writing poetry, competitive sports such as the Olympic games, universities, and a code of conduct for doctors.

But there are many differences, too. This book looks at some of the evidence for the Greek way of life, including pottery, buildings, tools and the informative works of philosophers and playwrights. Using the things that have been found, we can unravel the mystery of our past, to learn much about the ancient Greek way of life.

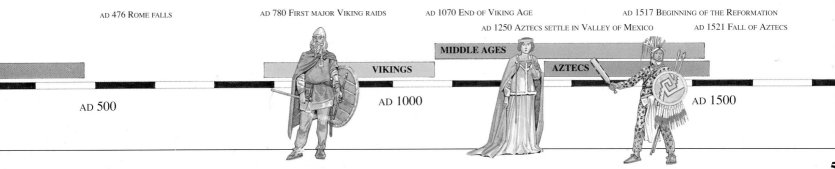

AD 476 ROME FALLS

AD 780 FIRST MAJOR VIKING RAIDS

AD 1070 END OF VIKING AGE

AD 1517 BEGINNING OF THE REFORMATION

AD 1250 AZTECS SETTLE IN VALLEY OF MEXICO

AD 1521 FALL OF AZTECS

MIDDLE AGES

VIKINGS

AZTECS

AD 500

AD 1000

AD 1500

HISTORY IN EVIDENCE

The work of historians and archaeologists helps us learn about the past. By studying evidence, they find out how people lived and worked, and what happened to them. For example, we have many texts written by scholars, playwrights and statesmen. From these written accounts we can learn about tremendous battles, the policies of government and the more simple events of everyday life.

We can also learn things from artifacts that are dug out of the ground. In many countries, the remains of vases and pots are evidence for widespread trade. Many of these artifacts are beautifully decorated with life-like scenes. For example, a vase might be painted with an agricultural scene or with details of a gory battle. From this pictorial information we can tell much about Greek food, fashion, warfare and the gods, myths and legends.

Written evidence has survived in several forms, such as the inscription on this bronze tablet (right). It is a treaty between two Greek cities.

Doric

There were three main styles of Greek architecture. The Doric style has a plain top, or capital. Ionic has a scrolled top like a ram's horn. The Corinthian style has a much more elaborate capital.

Ionic

Corinthian

Pottery was one of the main Greek exports. The painted scenes show many aspects of Greek life. On this vase, made in Athens in about 500 BC, young men are collecting water from a fountain.

Archaeologists use a wide range of tools in their work – from buckets, trowels and brushes for removing soil, to measures, laptop computers and cameras for recording the position of finds.

Throughout history, people have been fascinated by the achievements of the ancient Greeks, and many sites (right) have been excavated. Since about 1870, much more care has been taken to record finds carefully, and to study whole sites, not just individual buildings.

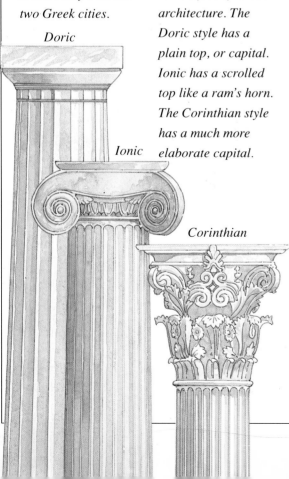

There are also hundreds of ancient buildings and statues. Wood and timber was in short supply, so large and important buildings were usually made of stone. Some of these structures, such as the Acropolis in Athens, have survived almost intact. If you have the chance to visit Greece, remember that these buildings were once painted in bright colors, like those shown in this book's scenes. Many of them were also decorated with stone carvings called reliefs, which show scenes of Greek life, their gods and heroes.

And it is not always necessary to visit Greece to see these treasures. Many of the great ancient Greek works of art are on display in museums throughout the world, where they can be seen by the public. And who knows what other buildings and artifacts are still to be discovered, to reveal more about our past?

The relief above was part of the decoration on the Parthenon at Athens, a temple to the goddess Athena.

The buildings of Greece (left) reflect its rich history – from ancient homes and temples (bottom), the churches and forts of the Byzantine empire (center), to windmills, houses and modern tower blocks (top).

The discovery of a coin, like this silver tetradrachm from Athens (circa 450 BC), can help to date a site. However, the coin could have been dug in lower or dropped later than its date would suggest.

A GREEK HOME

A house was home to many people – a husband, his wife and their children, their slaves and perhaps to some of the family's relatives. The man was head of the family. He was in charge of everyone within the home, including servants and slaves.

When a baby was born, the father decided if the child was healthy enough to be accepted: if not, the baby was left to die outside. The father chose a husband for his daughters and was able to disinherit a son who behaved badly. In Athens, people were citizens of the city only if their parents were also married citizens. Therefore most people married within a close group of relatives. When the head of the family died, his property was divided between all his surviving sons.

The wife's job was to bring up the children, to cook and to weave cloth. Otherwise, women had very little independence. They had to be protected by a guardian at all times, and they rarely left the house: when they did go out, they were not allowed to spend much money.

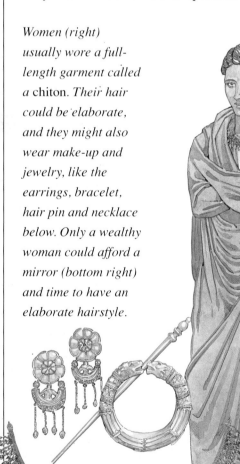

Women (right) usually wore a full-length garment called a chiton. Their hair could be elaborate, and they might also wear make-up and jewelry, like the earrings, bracelet, hair pin and necklace below. Only a wealthy woman could afford a mirror (bottom right) and time to have an elaborate hairstyle.

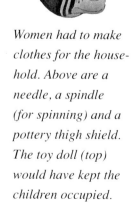

Women had to make clothes for the household. Above are a needle, a spindle (for spinning) and a pottery thigh shield. The toy doll (top) would have kept the children occupied.

In many older cities, only the grand public buildings were clean. Most houses were small and the streets were dirty and smelly. Priene was a newer city and was planned more carefully. Wealthy families (above) had homes with bathrooms.

8

The women drew out tufts of wool over a shield on their leg before spinning the wool. This vase (left) shows a woman holding a distaff in her left hand while the thread is pulled out and twisted by the spindle hanging below it.

The scene above shows women of a wealthy family who live in a large house in the city of Priene. The women are weaving at a loom in the loom room, which was one of the largest – the main room was where men met in the evenings. The women have washed, combed and dyed the wool, then spun it into a thread. In the courtyard, children play while servants work busily. In Athens in the early 5th century, there were about 60,000 slaves, that is one-third of the population.

Boys were taught lessons at home by a tutor or sent to a small private school – the girls had to learn to run the household. The boys were taught to read and write, some basic arithmetic, and how to play a musical instrument. Physical exercise was also part of their daily school routine.

A popular game played by women and children was knucklebones, shown in the terracotta model above. Each player had to throw small bones in the air and catch them on the back of their hand. People also played games with dice.

RURAL LIFE

ATTICA 455 BC

Life in the country was very
hard. Away from the river
plains, the land was rocky and the
soil of poor quality, so few crops
could be grown there. In the
mountains, terraced fields had to
be dug out of the hillsides. The
main crops were olives, grapes
and, in the plains, wheat.

The scene above shows countryside
in Attica, the region around Athens.
Workers are harvesting olives, which
will provide oil for cooking, for burning
in lamps and for cleaning the skin when
bathing. They are shaking and beating
the olives from the trees. Two men are
then using a press to squeeze the oil out.
The oil will be stored in jars called
amphorae, and some of it will be sold in
the towns and cities. Grapes were also
harvested and pressed in a similar way,
and the juice made into wine.

*The scene painted
on this vase (from
the 6th century BC)
shows workers
harvesting olives.
The men used long
sticks to knock down
the olives, so they
could be gathered for
eating or pressing.*

*The woman in this
stone carving (far
left) is picking fruit
called pomegranates.
The main meal of the
day was usually
followed by fruit.
Most food had to be
carried to the towns
on donkeys (top).
The rider in this
terracotta model is
seated on two large
cheeses! The bronze
strainer (above) was
used to strain wine or
other liquid.*

The young hunter painted on this vase is heavily armed with spears. He might be after a wild boar, rabbits or birds. He is wearing a short cloak and a felt hat to keep the fierce sun off his head.

In mountainous regions, farmers had to keep hardy, sure-footed goats (below) and sheep rather than cattle.

This terracotta model (left) shows a woman grinding grain. Even in the cities, people had to make their own bread – they could not buy ready-made loaves at the market.

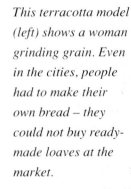

Olive oil was one of Attica's main exports. Once collected, the olives were pulped by hand. Then the juice was squeezed from them in large presses like the one shown on this 5th century bowl. The same device could be used for pressing grapes.

On the left of the scene, an elderly shepherd is watching his sheep, while on the right a goat and pigs forage for food. Farmers kept goats mainly for their milk and sheep for their wool. Meat was eaten only at festivals and when animals were sacrificed. On the right there's also a hunter and his dog.

Other important industries were forestry, fishing and weaving. The demand for wood for furniture, ships and buildings was so heavy that many areas suffered soil erosion. In the fourth century BC, the Athenian philosopher Plato described the damage:

'... what now remains... is like the bony body of a sick man, with all the rich and fertile earth fallen away and only the scraggy skeleton of the land left.'

The Greeks ate only one main meal, in the late afternoon. Breakfast and lunch were usually just snacks. This terracotta model shows a woman cooking a meal – only poorer families did not have slaves to help with the work.

THE MARKET PLACE

ATHENS 405 BC

Most of a town's important activities took place in the *agora*. This was a large open area which was usually in the centre of the town. There, men would gather to discuss politics, their business matters or simply to discuss everyday affairs.

At Athens, the *agora* was surrounded by the council building, the law courts, the mint and two great temples. The *agora* was also the market place. In the cool early morning the market would come to life with people setting up their stalls. Farmers came from the countryside to sell their produce and animals. Craftsmen tried to sell the things they had made.

Pottery came in many shapes and sizes, and was sold throughout the Mediterranean. The items below are perfume pots. The smaller, simpler one shows a winged man. The larger novelty pot (left) was made in Corinth.

A wide variety of goods was on sale at the market. The dice (top) were made of ivory, while the snake arm bracelet and fibula (above) were made of gold.

Only wealthy people could afford an ornate bronze oil lamp (right), instead of the common clay ones.

In the scene above, a market is full of busy people. The women are probably from poorer families. They have to leave their house because they do not have servants to do their shopping. On the left, a trader from Corinth is trying to sell his novelty pots and vessels. His customer will try to strike a hard bargain. Although there were no banks, a person could borrow from a money lender, like the one seated near the statue. People did use silver coins for buying goods, but it was also possible to barter for some items. Also present in the market might be one of the city's officials, checking that traders are giving people the correct weights and measures! From time to time there would be sales of slaves. Most slaves were not Greeks. They were usually captured in foreign lands and sold to the highest bidder. Not everyone could afford to own a slave as a servant. Slaves had to do shopping, household chores, work in the fields or, worse still, go down the mines (see page 16).

Greek merchants traded with Egypt and other African countries. This pot, made in about 250 BC, shows a person from south of Egypt, which Greek kings ruled at the time.

Many people worked in and around the agora. Below is a terracotta model of a barber at work, cutting a customer's hair. In the 6th century, craftsmen in Boeotia made many models of people going about their daily work.

The remains of the agora at Athens include the city's council chamber (the bouleuterion), mint and long buildings called stoa, where market stalls could be set up. There were also law courts, and large temples to Apollo (the god of music and oracles) and Hephaistos (the handicapped god of metalwork).

The Athenian council looked after a set of official bronze and lead weights (above). They were the city's standard weights, so officials could check that traders were selling the right amount of goods.

Athens also had official measures for the volume of grain and liquids such as oil and wine. The agora was a lively place when customers thought they had been short-changed!

Goods were often brought to market by donkey. This model shows how large baskets were strapped on either side of the animal.

LAST VOYAGE

Many of the goods sold in a town's market came from other regions. Athens had to import most of the grain it needed to feed its population, as well as timber for ships, furs and hides, iron, copper, papyrus and linen. In return, it traded olive oil, pottery, metalwork and honey.

Some goods were carried overland using donkeys. But it was dangerous crossing the mountains, so the Greeks relied on boats to travel around the islands of the Mediterranean. Even sailing close to the coast could be dangerous, because storms would spring up suddenly, or pirates attack.

In the main scene we can see a Greek trading vessel in an island harbor. Archaeological evidence can tell us a great deal about how a boat like this was built and sailed.

About 10,000 almonds (right) were found in the wreck. They had probably been grown in Cyprus in about 309 BC. The cargo also included grinding stones like the one below, used for crushing grain to make flour.

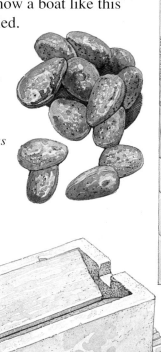

Over 400 amphorae (left) were part of the cargo. Although their contents have not survived, they would have contained olive oil or wine, sealed in with a clay plug.

In the wreck there were several articles belonging to the crew, such as this pitcher, oil jug and plate (right). Much of this pottery was made on the island of Rhodes, which could have been the ship's home port. The finds suggest that the ship had a crew of four.

The wreck was found in 1967 in about 100 feet of water, near Kyrenia in Cyprus. Over 5,000 pieces of the ship's timber were lifted for study and conservation.

This wooden block (above) was used to raise the wooden spar that held the sail. The sail would have been furled and unfurled like a huge Venetian blind, using ropes running through lead rings (top).

Archaeologists found that the outside of the wooden hull had been covered in lead sheeting (above). The lead protected the hull timbers from attack by shipworm. The hull would also have been painted with soot and pitch. This was to keep seaweed from growing on the ship and slowing it down.

Archaeologists have found one very important shipwreck, with its cargo, off the coast of Cyprus. The ship was over 40 feet long and was built from pine. Its hull was covered in lead to protect it from shipworms. Scientists have used carbon-14 dating to show the ship was built in about 389 BC. It is thought that the ship was 80 years old when she sank. Perhaps pirates attacked the ship, seized her crew as slaves, then made holes in the hull to sink her.

The underwater excavation revealed that the boat's cargo included over 400 amphorae. Piled within the hull were thousands of almonds, whose sacks had rotted away long ago. Using the surviving timbers as a plan, a full-scale replica of the ship has been built and sailed in the Mediterranean Sea.

MINING FOR METAL

LAURIUM 350 BC

In 482 BC, a rich seam of silver was found in hills at Laurium, in Attica. The citizens of Athens were persuaded by one of the city's leaders, Themistocles, to use this new-found wealth to build a fleet of warships. As a result, Athens became the leading Greek city-state in the 5th century BC. Most of its great power and wealth came from trade and the large navy it had built.

Two of Greece's major industries were mining and metal working. As well as the silver at Laurium, the Greeks mined gold, copper (from Cyprus), iron and lead, all of which were used to make useful and beautiful tools, weapons and jewelry. The Greeks also quarried marble and limestone for buildings.

Talented craftsmen could make beautiful objects in a range of metals. This griffin head (below) was cast from bronze, a mixture of copper and tin. The griffin is a mythical creature from Greek legends.

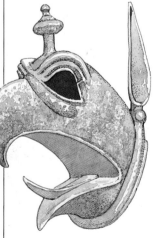

This beautiful gold earring (above) dates from about the 3rd century BC. The goldsmith who made it must have spent many hours on the fine chains, angels and other intricate decoration.

Shown above are archaeological remains of the ore wash at a silver mine at Laurium in Attica.

Still preserved at Laurium are the shallow wells used for cleaning the ore and the channels in which the water flowed.

These mines and quarries were controlled by the city governments and worked by slave labor. At Laurium, as many as 20,000 slaves were employed. Deep below ground, they worked long hours in harsh conditions. Down on their hands and knees, miners used crude picks and chisels to break off the rock, which was then hauled to the surface in baskets, often carried by children. There was little ventilation so it was very hot and very dirty. The playwright Euripides wrote of the plight of slaves:

'Slavery, that thing of evil, by its nature [is] evil, forcing submission from man to what no man should yield to.'

The scene on the left shows slaves crushing the ore into small lumps and then washing it in water. This separated the heavy ore from the lighter dust and waste material. The ore was then heated in a fire called a furnace, to extract the metal, a mixture of lead and silver. The silver was then heated again, in a special container, to separate it from the lead.

The Greeks produced coins as early as the 7th century BC. Most were made of silver. The ones shown here depict a bull, a shield, the goddess Athena, the winged horse Pegasus and an apple!

The decorated silver bowl (right), made in the 5th century BC, was discovered in southern France. It is a libation bowl for holding an offering of wine or other liquid for a god or goddess. Silver is a quite soft metal, so it can be worked easily.

The back of this bronze mirror (below) shows Aphrodite, goddess of beauty, and Pan, the god of woods, fields and shepherds.

In this vase painting (above), a metalworker is holding a piece of hot metal with a pair of tongs. He is shaping it with a hammer held high in his other hand. His furnace is probably heated with charcoal, and will only be hot enough to soften the metal, not melt it.

The miners in this painted clay tablet (right) are able to stand upright – in the real mines, they had to kneel to work. Guards were posted at the entrance to stop slaves escaping.

THE BATTLE OF MARATHON

MARATHON 490 BC

Greek states were constantly under attack from their Greek neighbors and peoples from other lands. Because of this, most states raised a strong army. Some armies had cavalry, slingers and javelin-throwers. But the main soldiers were the hoplites, named after their weapons and armor, *hopla*. Hoplites carried a strong round shield and many wore metal armor and helmets. They usually fought with a long spear or sword and a short dagger.

In the 5th century BC, the Greeks' greatest enemy was Persia. In 490 BC the Persian army invaded Greece, and came face-to-face with Athenian and Plataian hoplites at a place called Marathon. The Greeks had never before defeated a Persian army, and so at first were very reluctant to attack! However, the Greek soldiers fought bravely, and when the Persians fled to their ships (shown in the main scene) they had left 6,400 dead behind them. The Athenians had lost only 192 men.

The two bowls below are painted with military scenes. The large bowl (called a krater) has two soldiers leaving for war, armed with long spears and round shields. The panel from a bowl below it shows a wounded soldier being aided by one of his comrades.

The Greeks advanced when the Persian cavalry was away from the battlefield, and cleverly attacked around the wings of the Persian army. After the battle, the 192 dead Athenian soldiers were buried in a communal grave with earth heaped over them (above). The mound was excavated in 1897.

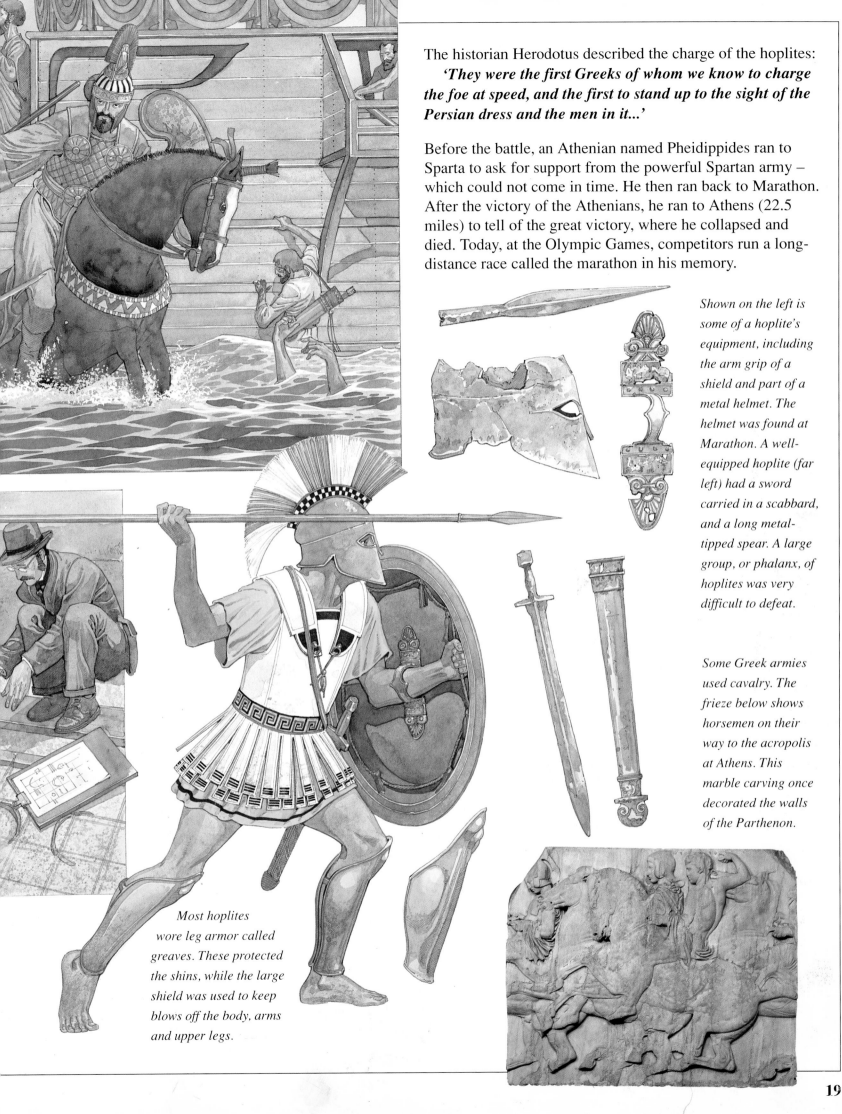

The historian Herodotus described the charge of the hoplites:
'They were the first Greeks of whom we know to charge the foe at speed, and the first to stand up to the sight of the Persian dress and the men in it...'

Before the battle, an Athenian named Pheidippides ran to Sparta to ask for support from the powerful Spartan army – which could not come in time. He then ran back to Marathon. After the victory of the Athenians, he ran to Athens (22.5 miles) to tell of the great victory, where he collapsed and died. Today, at the Olympic Games, competitors run a long-distance race called the marathon in his memory.

Shown on the left is some of a hoplite's equipment, including the arm grip of a shield and part of a metal helmet. The helmet was found at Marathon. A well-equipped hoplite (far left) had a sword carried in a scabbard, and a long metal-tipped spear. A large group, or phalanx, of hoplites was very difficult to defeat.

Some Greek armies used cavalry. The frieze below shows horsemen on their way to the acropolis at Athens. This marble carving once decorated the walls of the Parthenon.

Most hoplites wore leg armor called greaves. These protected the shins, while the large shield was used to keep blows off the body, arms and upper legs.

PHILOSOPHY AND MEDICINE

The Greeks are famous for their philosophy. For men, a part of everyday life was to sit in the shade, away from the direct heat of the sun, and discuss the world around them. They tried to explain the meaning of the things and understand the events they saw. The ideas of some philosophers, such as Plato and Aristotle, are still studied today.

The Greeks studied many branches of learning, such as mathematics and astronomy, and set up the world's first universities. They also studied medicine. People still worshiped the gods of healing, Asclepius and Apollo, but many doctors were treated like skilled craftsmen. They all had to treat a wide variety of ailments, whereas people now specialize in particular areas, such as dentistry, surgery and physiotherapy.

Plato (left) was a pupil of Socrates. He wrote a book, The Republic, *with ideas on how governments should run an ideal state, and how people should treat each other.*

Aristotle (right) was interested in solving practical problems. He divided learning into subjects like biology and physics. His ideas led to the study of logic, the rules of thinking.

Socrates posed his students many questions aimed at getting a clearer understanding of the world. Aged 70, he was prosecuted for corrupting the minds of the young and sentenced to death.

The philosopher and mathematician Pythagoras (right) is most famous for his theorem explaining the relationship between the sides of a right-angled triangle ($a^2 = b^2 + c^2$).

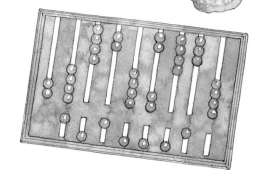

Mathematicians and traders did sums on an abacus (left). The counters represented the units – ones, tens, hundreds, etc.

Patients who had been cured made offerings to thank their gods or doctors. This offering (left), a stone carving, is called a votive relief. It shows a man named Lysimachides, whose leg had been cured by a doctor called Amynos.

This votive relief (right), dating from the 4th century BC, shows a doctor treating a person who has been bitten by a snake.

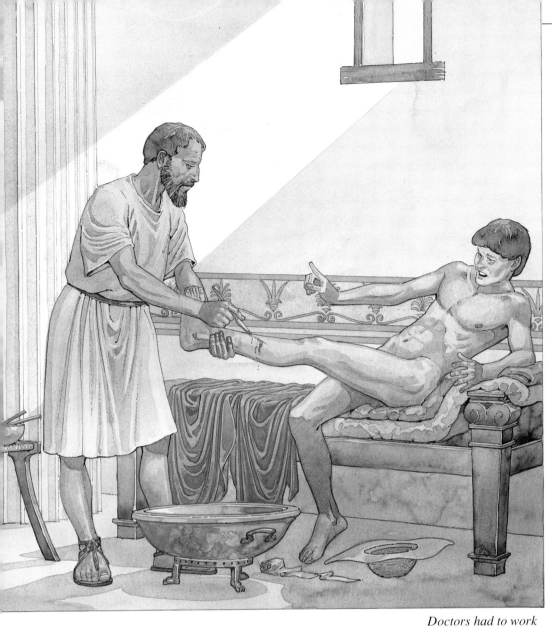

However, Greek doctors did not know very much about illnesses. Their treatments usually consisted of providing a good diet, keeping the patient comfortable, and exercise.

The most famous Greek doctor was Hippocrates. He did not think that every illness had to be treated in the same way. Instead, he believed each problem had a separate cause and remedy. He also said that doctors must have high standards, and follow a code of conduct:

'I swear by Apollo ... I will not give to anyone any medicine which will kill or harm them...Whatever I see or hear, I shall not tell anyone.'

Today, doctors take an oath, called the Hippocratic Oath, which is similar to the one his followers had to swear.

Doctors had to work with relatively simple instruments, such as scalpels and probes (below). The Greeks did not believe in cutting up dead bodies, so doctors did not know very much about anatomy. Ointments were ground and mixed from ingredients such as minerals, herbs and honey.

Many people believed that Asclepius (left), a legendary doctor who was worshiped as a god, could cure their ailments. Hippocrates (above) was the greatest of all Greek physicians.

AT THE THEATER

Epidauros 300 BC

Two thousand years ago, there were no hi-tech communications which brought entertainment directly to people's homes. Instead, Greeks had to entertain themselves with drinking parties, games, pets and festivals. In Athens, people could go to see 'magicians' and jugglers doing tricks in the *agora*, or visit the public baths.

However, the most important entertainments were also religious festivals held in honor of the gods and goddesses. For example, going to the theater was an important part of a festival to the god Dionysus. It was a very popular choice with citizens, and plays were always well attended by poor as well as rich people. In Athens, Pericles' government paid for productions, and sometimes for people to see them!

This terracotta statue shows two comic actors. All actors wore masks.

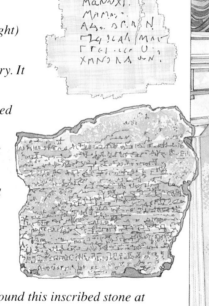

This papyrus (right) is a very rare fragment of poetry. It was written by a female poet named Sappho who wrote about love, and the joy and suffering it can bring.

Archaeologists found this inscribed stone at Delphi. It shows the words of a song, with the musical score to accompany them. It is the oldest known musical score.

Epidauros had stone stage buildings (left). Most of the action took place in an open area called the orchestra. The audience of up to 14,000 people was seated on steep banks, radiating out from the orchestra.

The statuette below shows Melpomene, one of the nine Greek muses. The muses were goddesses, and each represented an art form, such as music, poetry, dance and acting.

These three masks (above and right) represent a good and happy character, a sad or tragic one, and an angry person. The exaggerated features could be seen more clearly than an actor's face.

Greek plays were often accompanied by music and sometimes by singers. Music was played on instruments such as cymbals, flute and lyre (left). Music was an important part of a play, because it could be used to emphasize happy, sad or tragic moments.

In the main scene actors are performing a play, accompanied by musicians. Women were not allowed to act in plays, so all the parts were played by men. The actors did not have many props to help them explain the plot. However, they all wore masks to show the audience whether a character was happy or sad. The shape of a theater was like a bowl, so that all the words and sounds could be heard clearly by the audience.

Talented playwrights were highly thought of, and some became very famous outside Greece. The texts of many Greek plays have survived to the present time, so people can still enjoy the works of writers such as Sophocles, Aristophanes and Euripides.

TEMPLES AND GODS

OLYMPIA 432 BC

Many people know about the Olympic Games, but not so many know that the games were held to honor the mighty Zeus, chief of the gods. In about 438 BC, the council at Olympia commissioned a gigantic new statue of him for their temple.

The statue (shown in the scene on the right) was built by a sculptor called Pheidias. It was so magnificent that it became known as one of the seven wonders of the world. Today only the remains of the base within the temple have survived. Other evidence includes coins that depict the colossal Zeus, and debris of ivory, metal, glass and terracotta molds found in the remains of a nearby workshop.

However, there are several descriptions of the statue. In the first century AD, a Greek geographer called Strabo wrote: *'[The sculptor] has shown Zeus seated, but with his head almost touching the ceiling, so we have the impression that if Zeus moved to stand up, he would unroof the temple.'*

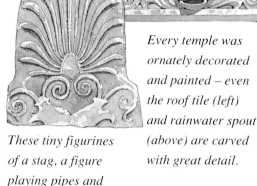

Every temple was ornately decorated and painted – even the roof tile (left) and rainwater spout (above) are carved with great detail.

These tiny figurines of a stag, a figure playing pipes and Artemis (goddess of wild animals and hunting), were made to please the gods.

This bronze head shows the goddess Aphrodite. She was the goddess of love, beauty and fertility.

Pheidias also made a colossal gold and ivory statue of the war goddess Athena, who represented justice. The marble copy (left) is Roman, from about AD 130.

Greeks worshiped heroes like Icarus (top) who flew too close to the sun with his wings of feathers and wax, and Hercules (above), famed for his strength and bravery.

Archaeologists have uncovered the site of Zeus' temple at Olympia (right), and also the workshop of Pheidias, described by Pausanius in the second century AD.

A century later, Pausanius wrote:

' On his right hand he holds a figure of Victory made of ivory and gold... In his left hand the god holds his scepter inlaid with every kind of metal, and the bird perched on the scepter is an eagle.'

As well as Zeus, Greeks worshiped many other gods and heroes. They believed there was a god for all aspects of the world, who could be pleased by sacrifices of food and animals. For instance, they would make a sacrifice to the god of war, Ares, before a battle. When things went wrong in life, people thought that the gods were angry, and that they were being punished.

No special qualifications were needed to become a priest—it was a part-time job. The only people who had full-time religious jobs were seers. They interpreted the will of the gods from signs such as birds flying or the entrails of sacrificed animals.

These chisels and clay mold were found in the remains of the workshop. Pausanius said of Zeus:'his garments are carved with animals and lily flowers.'

Greek coins often depicted well-known statues. Zeus was shown on this coin from the state of Elis.

THE OLYMPIC GAMES

Every four years, international sports men and women compete in the Olympic Games. The first games were held by the ancient Greeks at Olympia in honor of Zeus. We know about the festival of games through written accounts and artifacts decorated with scenes of the competitors.

The games were so important that a sacred two-month truce was called. During this truce, competitors and thousands of spectators could travel safely to and from Olympia.

Each festival began with priests sacrificing sheep or cattle on a great altar to Zeus. The animals' blood was caught in a bowl and poured on the altar, their entrails were read for omens, and the meat was eaten. Then the athletes swore oaths to Zeus, and the games began.

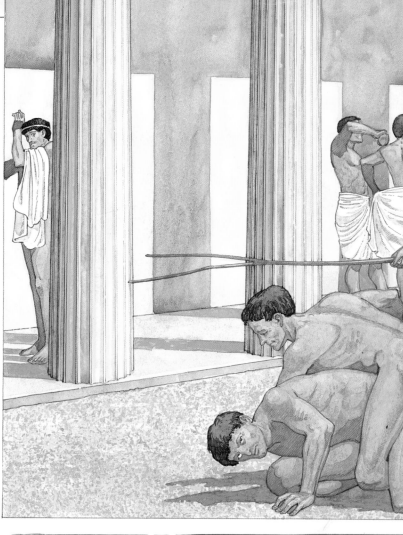

Above is a bronze discus. Its inscription says that it was used by an athlete called Exoidas when he won the competition. Alongside it is a weight used in long jump. Greek long-jumpers carried a weight in each hand, which they swung to help them go further.

The scene painted on this vase shows athletes competing in the pentathlon. The pentathlon was a combination of five events: long jump, discus, javelin, wrestling and running one length of the stadium, over 200 yards.

The beautifully crafted bronze statue above shows a discus thrower. Only men could compete in the games; women had their own games in honor of Hera, the wife of Zeus.

This small gold medal (far left) was awarded to one of the winners, along with a garland of olive leaves. The scene beside it depicts a pig being sacrificed. Religious events took up over two days of the festival.

The magnificent sculpture below, which shows two wrestlers, is one of the finest pieces of Greek art. The best Greek sculptors could produce figures that were accurate and beautiful when seen from any angle.

This fine stone carving on the base of a statue (above) shows Olympic events. In the center are two wrestlers, watched by judges. Wrestling was very popular and also quite dangerous.

As well as a religious festival, the games were a social and political gathering. The occasion was a happy one, like a fair, with people selling goods, food and drink. Archaeologists have found the remains of many buildings at Olympia, preserved by a landslide and mud that covered the site. There are no remains of houses, which suggests that people slept in tents.

There were fewer events than in the modern games. Horse and chariot races were followed by the pentathlon. In the main scene we can see wrestlers practicing for their bouts, with the judges gathered around them. Other sports included boys' events, plus the 200 meters, 400 meters and a longer race. On the last day there was more wrestling, plus boxing and *pankration*, a vicious form of fighting with very few rules! The last event was a running race in full armor. Finally, at the end of the week, there were a banquet and more sacrifices.

A ROYAL TOMB

VERGINA 336 BC

One of the most famous ancient Greek leaders was Alexander the Great, the son of Philip II of Macedon. At the age of 20, Alexander led his army to victory against Persia and conquered a huge empire, eventually reaching as far as India. Alexander died of malaria in 323 BC. He was only 32 years old.

Ancient historians wrote about the exploits of Alexander and his powerful father. In the 4th century, Philip had conquered Athens and the other Greek states. However, his tomb had never been found. Then, in 1977, a Greek archaeologist discovered a building inside an ancient mound. The building, which had two small chambers under a curved roof, had been sealed for 23 centuries, and had not been plundered by robbers. Was this the royal tomb of Philip II?

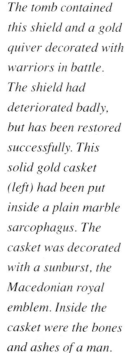

These greaves (leg armor) were found in the tomb. Although a pair, they are of different sizes. Had they belonged to Philip II?

The tomb contained this shield and a gold quiver decorated with warriors in battle. The shield had deteriorated badly, but has been restored successfully. This solid gold casket (left) had been put inside a plain marble sarcophagus. The casket was decorated with a sunburst, the Macedonian royal emblem. Inside the casket were the bones and ashes of a man.

The tomb was a dramatic find, even though any items made of wood had perished – the armor on the floor had once stood on a wooden couch. The main scene shows Alexander watching his father's effects being placed in the inner chamber of the tomb.

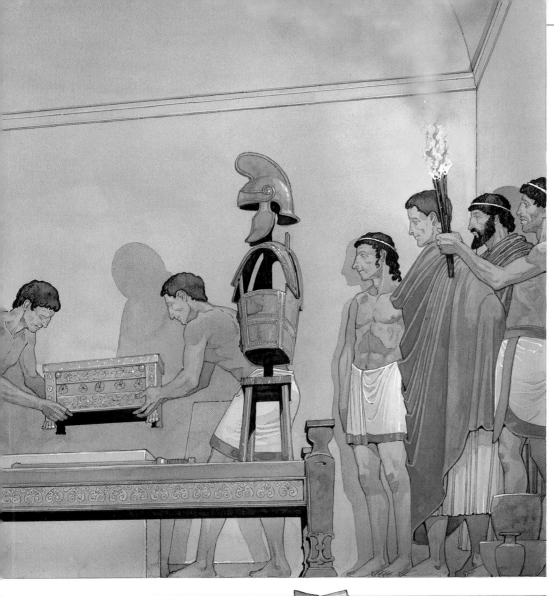

The walls of the tomb were not richly painted, unlike many other royal tombs. Philip had been assassinated at his daughter's wedding, so his sudden death meant that there had not been much time for extravagant decoration. Philip's body would have been cremated, and his bones and ashes placed in a golden casket.

Also, many of the items in the tomb could have belonged to Philip. In particular, there is a pair of greaves, armor worn on the lower part of the leg. Although of the same design, one is a different shape to the other. It is known that Philip was lame in one leg, so might have needed greaves like this.

The ivory bust above was found in the outer chamber. It is similar to a portrait on a medallion (above right) which shows Philip wearing a jeweled head-band called a diadem. A diadem (top) was found in the tomb.

This small bronze vase was one of many silver, gold, bronze and iron vessels in the two chambers of the small royal tomb.

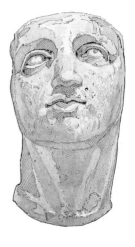

Also in the outer chamber was this bust, believed to be of Alexander. The head is shown tilted, like many other portraits of Alexander. When he became king of Macedon and Greece, Alexander launched a devastating invasion of Persia, defeating the Persian king Darius.

29

GLOSSARY

This list explains the meaning of some of the words and terms used in the book.

AMPHORA

ACROPOLIS   A collection of buildings built as a safe haven on high ground. The acropolis at Athens had been a fortress but became the site of two temples to Athena (the Parthenon and Erectheion) and a magnificent gateway (the Propylaea).

AGORA   A large open space, usually situated in the center of a town, used for the open-air market and public meetings.

AMPHORA   A two-handled pottery container for storing goods.

ARCHAEOLOGIST   A person who finds, studies and conserves the remains of past civilizations.

ARTIFACT   An object from the past that has been made by people.

BARTER   To exchange goods for something other than money.

CITIZEN   A free person who has rights in their own city or region.

CITY-STATE   A small country controlled by a powerful city.

COLONY   A new settlement or country set up by people who have left their homeland.

DEMOCRACY   A method of government that involves a large part of the population. For example, all adult males in Athens could vote to elect the city's leader.

HOPLITE   A heavily-armed foot soldier. Greek hoplites often fought in large, disciplined groups called phalanxes.

IVORY   The tusk of an elephant or hippopotamus.

MINOANS   An ancient civilization of approximately 2200-1400 BC, who lived on the island of Crete.

MYCENAEAN   An early civilization of ancient Greece.

OATH   A promise. The Hippocratic Oath, sworn by doctors, is a promise to treat people properly and fairly.

ORE   A rocky mixture that contains metals such as lead or silver.

PHILOSOPHER   A person who tries to understand the meaning of the world around them, and how people behave.

QUARRY   A place where stone is cut out of the ground.

RELIEF   A scene or pattern carved out of stone or wood.

SACRIFICE   Killing animals or giving up belongings as an offering to a goddess or god.

SLAVE   A person who is owned by another person, and has very few rights.

SPARTA   A powerful city in southern Greece. Sparta was famous for its soldiers, trained from birth.

STATE   A small, independent country, usually controlled by a powerful city.

TERRACOTTA   Baked clay, used for making pottery and small statuettes.

HOPLITE

PHILOSOPHER

KEY DATES

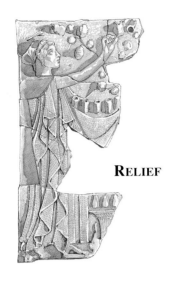

RELIEF

SACRIFICE

c2000 BC	Arrival on mainland Greece of first Greek-speaking people.
c1700-1200	Mycenaean civilization in Greece.
c1200-800	Greek Dark Ages. First Greek settlements on coast of Asia Minor.
800-500	Archaic period.
776	First Olympic Games.
750-700	Development of Greek alphabet. Soldiers begin to fight as hoplites.
730	Rise of Corinth as leading city.
c700	New colonies include Sybaris (720), Kyrene (630) and Massalia (600).
621	The statesman Draco makes the first written laws in Athens.
500-300	Classical period.
493	Themistocles becomes leader of Athens.
490	First Persian invasion under Darius. Battle of Marathon.
482	Discovery of silver at Laurium.
480	Persians invade mainland Greece under Xerxes. Battles at Thermopylae and Salamis, and Plataea (479)
461	Pericles leads Athens, until 429. Athens at war with Sparta until 451.
451	Athens passes law defining who is a citizen.
447	Work begins on Parthenon.
c430	Hippocrates and Socrates active, Pheidias sculpts statue of Zeus.
425-405	Playwrights Euripides, Aristophanes and Sophocles popular.
404	Decline of Athens, Sparta becomes leading city-state.
400-360	Plato active.
358	Works starts on theater at Epidauros.
338	Philip II of Macedon conquers Athens.
336	Philip II dies. His son Alexander 'the Great' becomes king and conquers Asia Minor, Egypt, Mesopotamia and parts of India.
335	Aristotle, who had been Alexander's tutor, begins teaching in Athens.
323	Death of Alexander and break-up of his empire (by 311), although Greek kings still rule Egypt and Syria.
300-148	Hellenistic period.
325-300	The geographer Pytheas sails as far as Britain and perhaps Iceland.
260-215	Archimedes active.
148	Macedonia becomes a Roman province.

TERRACOTTA MODEL

QUOTATIONS

P. 4 Aristotle (c384-322 BC) wrote about democracy in his book *Politics*.
P. 11 The Greek landscape was described by Plato (c427-347 BC) in his book *Critias*. He probably exaggerated what was a serious problem for some farmers.
P. 17 The playwright Euripides (c480-430 BC) was one of the greatest writers of tragic poetry. His description of slavery comes from one of his plays. **P. 19** The historian Herodotus (c485-425 BC) described the Battle of Marathon in his *Histories*. **P. 21** Hippocrates (c460-377 BC) is known as the 'father of medicine'. The quotation is from *Hippocratic Precepts I*, possibly written by one of his followers. **P. 24** The quotation by Strabo (64 BC-AD 24), who traveled widely, comes from his *Geographical Sketches*. **P. 25** Pausanius (AD 143-176) described Olympia in his book *Descriptions of Greece*.

INDEX

DATE DUE

938
Jam

James, John
**How we know about the
Greeks**

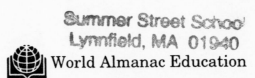 World Almanac Education

MEDIALOG INC
ALEXANDRIA KY 41001